FLAVOR

OF THE
MONTH

A LEADERSHIP FABLE

about management mantras,
methodologies, processes, &
practices. Learn what works in
the real world

Martin VanDerSchouw

LGd
Press

Flavor Of The Month

Published by LGd Press
4610 South Ulster St. Suite 150 Denver, CO 80237
www.lookingglassdev.com

LGd Press books and products are available through most bookstores. To contact LGd Press directly call our customer care department within the U.S. at 888-338-7447 or fax 303-600-0985

Library of Congress Cataloging-in-Publication Data

VanDerSchouw, Martin 1966-
Flavor of the Month: a leadership fable about management mantras, methodologies processes, & practices. Learn what works in the real world / Martin VanDerSchouw.
p. cm.
ISBN-13: 978-0-9821856-2-9
ISBN-10: 0-9821856-2-6
1. Leadership. 2. Organizational behavior. I Title: Flavor of the month.
Printed in the United States of America

CONTENTS

This book is dedicated to my best friend, my partner, and the love of my life. Thank you Amy for everything you do.

Reality

Jim Calvin asked his assistant Jenny to hold all his calls as he walked into his office. He needed time to think. It had been three months since Jim had taken over as the President and Chief Executive Officer of JenMar. The JenMar Board of Directors had hired him because of his successful four year tenure leading the largest division of Axom Global. Both companies were in the same market, but JenMar was about half the size of Axom. When Jim first got the job he thought it would be the opportunity of a lifetime. Now he wasn't so sure.

Jim's predecessor had led the company for fifteen years and was the son of JenMar's founder. He had started in the mail room and worked in almost every department before taking over for his father. JenMar had gone public five years ago and the Griswold family that had owned the company since it opened had given up controlling interest in hopes of rapid growth. JenMar's now public board had become increasingly dissatisfied with the organization's performance and six months prior to Jim's arrival they had asked Jim's predecessor to resign. Out of the six candidates that had been interviewed Jim had been selected. The Chair of the Selection Committee had told him that he had gotten the job because of two factors: his track record of turning similar organizations around and his knowledge of complex regulatory issues such as Sarbanes-Oxley.

Jim stood leaning over his credenza staring out at the Denver skyline. He had not come into the job blindly. Before Jim took the job he had done extensive research on JenMar. What he found did not surprise him. Like most companies, JenMar had some fantastic people who often succeeded in spite of the leadership and processes in place. Everyone claimed to have "*world class processes*", but very few Jim had found really had tested those claims. JenMar was no different. Many of the employees were frustrated, but the management team thought things were going pretty well. In fact, many of the senior management team felt a majority of the issues were localized to a few individual employees. As a company, JenMar had largely grown through the continuous acquisition of smaller organizations. Most of the acquisitions were justified using the guise of "*organizational synergies*" and "*cost efficiencies*".

Although most of JenMar's leadership believed they had done a good job of integrating these smaller firms into the JenMar family, the reality was quite different. Rarely had JenMar laid-off many workers from the acquired companies. Because 60%-70% of the costs in these businesses were labor only minimal costs savings were ever achieved in the acquisitions. In many ways, the acquired organizations still operated as if they were still separate companies further reducing the cost savings. The net effect of these purchases was to constantly increase JenMar's revenue. This of course made the shareholders happy, at least temporarily.

The problem was that in addition to increasing JenMar's revenues all those acquisitions had also significantly bloated the company's cost structure. The lag between the immediate boost in revenue and the newly absorbed expenses (about six months) allowed the balance sheet to look pretty good, at least until inevitably the economy slowed down.

This problem was not new. Jim recalled first discussing it at an executive conference several years ago. In that session the instructor drew a two line graph to highlight the trends in revenue and costs. As Jim thought back to the discussion he redrew the two S curves on a blank piece of paper sitting on his desk. The worst part of the image Jim recalled was the far right tail where the revenue line went flat because of factors such as markets simply not growing, product confusion, product obsolescence, the economy, and several other factors. The revenue line became flat while the cost line continued to climb till it caught up with revenue around six months later.

How Acquisitions Mislead

Revenue

Expenses

Time--->

Jim's revenue and cost drawing

Like almost everyone else, when the U.S. economy went into the recession JenMar had to tighten its belt. All of a sudden JenMar was working to drastically cut its costs and was not looking to acquire new companies. In the six months prior to Jim's arrival JenMar's costs had caught up with its revenues and the picture was not pretty. Jim's predecessor had made dramatic across the board cuts in almost every department's budget. The first things to go were most training and marketing efforts. All major software and equipment purchases had been put on hold as well. It hadn't helped.

By the time Jim got to JenMar all the typical cost reduction measures had been taken. Gone were the free soft drinks in the break room and the regular Friday bagel boxes. Travel had been significantly curtailed, and the annual corporate retreat to a sunny location had been cancelled. JenMar had even tried to off-shored most of its manufacturing to Mumbai.

The off-shore effort had been an especially costly misstep. The JenMar leadership team had expected their Mumbai partners to provide a level of process and managerial control similar to what JenMar was doing internally. JenMar's executive team was shocked when it did not happen and JenMar had to deal significant quality issues and schedule delays. All of this just added to the cost issues within the company.

None of these ideas had made the significant impact the Board desired. In a last ditch effort to save his job,

Jim's predecessor had deployed a PMO to focus the new products team, started an ITIL initiative to get the IT organization to focus more on delivering new services to the organization instead of just purchasing more hardware and software, and had asked the human resources organization to lead a lean initiative to find ways to streamline and improve the organization's processes.

When Jim arrived, he had quickly realized JenMar had no strategy for the cuts the management team was making. Each department had been asked to make a flat reduction without anyone thinking through how those cuts would impact other groups in the organization. Jim had learned long ago that cost cutting measures rarely worked when they were generic and across-the-board. One of Jim's first decisions was to stop all budgetary cutting until he and the leadership team had developed a strategy for where they wanted the company to go and how they were going to get there. Once the team had developed the strategy, Jim was able to make some major decisions.

One of the biggest decisions Jim had made was closing the Detroit facility. The facility had provided phone center and office support for the company. Over two decades ago the facility had unionized. The operational costs for Detroit were 23% higher than any other location JenMar operated and regularly achieved the lowest productivity rates. When Jim first came to JenMar he had tried to negotiate with the union leaders, but they did not seem to want to grasp the realities JenMar faced. They stridently refused to give on wages or benefits that were consistently the highest in the company. Sadly, many of the workers were now learning that a wage and benefits package that was lower and in line with the rest of the market would be preferable to no job at all.

Laying off the 650 workers at the facility was one of the hardest decisions Jim had ever made, but it was necessary if JenMar was to survive. Jim had personally travelled to Detroit to tell all the workers they were losing their jobs. That was the worst meeting Jim had ever run. As Jim recalled the meeting he also remembered the shocking encounter he had with one of the workers.

Jim had spent two hours answering questions in the meeting. Most of the employees were simply scared. They had no idea how they were going to feed their families without the job JenMar had provided for years. Some were very angry. Some of the anger was directed at Jim's predecessor, but a lot was directed at Jim and his management team. Those willing to share their anger accused JenMar's management of taking advantage of its workers.

One of the most important management lessons Jim had ever learned was the importance of leading by example. In the corporate world that meant never asking your people to make sacrifices you were unwilling to make. Many of the Detroit workers had been shocked to learn that Jim had reduced the salaries of all the senior leadership team by 20%, and that he was only being paid $100,000 per year, an 80% reduction from his predecessor. Any additional compensation was variable based upon quantitative objectives established by the Board. One of the objective criteria in his performance plan he informed the workers was employee satisfaction with the leadership team. Simply put, if the employees were not happy, and JenMar was not successful Jim would not be successful or happy either.

As Jim concluded the meeting and began walking off the stage several employees had come up to him to talk personally. Most were complimentary with the way Jim had handled the situation, but one woman was extremely upset. He still remembered her vividly. He only wished now that he had recognized her as a foreshadowing of the problems JenMar would later face.

When Debbie Curtis approached Jim at the end of the meeting she was crushed. She had worked for JenMar for 15 years. She could not believe her company was laying her off. She felt she was a good employee. She was on time and always got acceptable performance reviews. Although the look in her eyes saddened Jim, it was her rhetorical question that shocked him. When Debbie Curtis approached Jim that day she asked, "How could he close the facility? Didn't Jim understand

JenMar had an obligation to employ her and the other workers? Every company she continued had as its first responsibility providing good jobs to its workforce."

Jim did not want to get into an economic debate with Debbie, and had simply thanked her for her opinion, told her that he appreciated all her efforts for JenMar, and let her know how sorry he was it had come to this. But, as Jim walked to his car with his administrative assistant Jenny he couldn't help but think to himself, in a capitalist economy like the U.S. companies do not exist to provide for their workers. They exist to make money for the owners and/or shareholders. The sad economic truth is that if a company does not make money it goes out of business. Fortunately, most executives have learned over the years that the best way to make money is to take good care of your employees. The question was how to get JenMar back on its feet and making money in both the short and long term so he could take care of his employees.

Jim was confident the practices he had used before would work at JenMar. Every successful executive Jim knew was putting similar practices into place. When he and his leadership team pushed ahead with the Lean Initiative everyone seemed on board. Jim had brought in the best consultants money could buy. He had worked with his Chief Information Officer, Karen Dougen, to ensure the ITIL initiative that had been going on for almost a year would not be impacted, and with Chuck Kois, his PMO Director, to ensure the Program

Management Office would be supportive. Jim was sure the leadership team had done a good job focusing on getting buy-in throughout the organization.

Jim had just gotten back from a grueling three hour senior management meeting. The meeting had been set up months ago. It was suppose to be an hour long update by the external consultants. It had not worked out that way. Twenty minutes into the meeting everyone was arguing and talking over everyone else.

It all started when Catherine Jacobs, JenMar's Chief Operating Officer had presented the results of the organizational survey designed to show the results of their Lean efforts. The numbers were not encouraging. Most of the organization had lost faith in the improvement efforts and many had fallen back into their old habits and processes. There was strong evidence that the Lean Initiative was conflicting with both information technology's ITIL efforts and the Program Management Office's implementation initiative. Each initiative leader had taken the position that their initiative should be the dominant effort for JenMar. Worst of all, most of the early performance gains had been lost and only 23% of the employees believed management intended on follow through with promised changes.

Jim stared out his window at the snowcapped peaks of the Colorado Rocky Mountains. The view always helped him think. JenMar had some of the most talented people Jim had ever met. Why was the company always late with new products, struggling with quality issues, and seeing inconsistent results at best? There had to be an answer. Jim's job was depending on it.

Just then Catherine Jacobs walked in and asked if she could have a few minutes to talk about next steps. Jim pointed to the burgundy leather sofa and easy chair in one corner of his office as he said, "sure". He could tell Catherine was just as frustrated as he was.

"Catherine, do you think it is possible that we are trying to change too much, too quickly?" Jim asked.

Catherine thought for a minute, and then answered. "I guess it's possible. After all, people tend to resist change, and we are trying to change a lot of things here. But, many of the efforts were started and were failing before you or I got here. I thought we had been making good progress getting things back on track until we got the survey results." Before Jim could add anything, Catherine quickly added, "I think we need to give it more time. We can have several more resources here on Monday and we will re-double our efforts."

Months later Jim would recount that this was the moment when it hit him. The reality was that JenMar was on the verge of becoming another statistic. What was it his long-time friend Ken Collier had told him, "Seven out of ten process improvement initiatives fail within one year, and on average these initiatives cost their organizations more than $750,000." They were pretty close to owing their consultants that now weren't they? Jim looked at Catherine and said, "We need help. I know someone who was walking me through a situation similar to ours a few months ago. I just didn't know it back then. I am going to get him in here. Are you free for lunch on Wednesday?" Catherine nodded she was. Jim ended the meeting and headed back to his desk to make a phone call.

Ken answered on the second ring. After hearing Jim's situation, Ken was more than happy to come in for lunch on Wednesday. More importantly, Ken thought he could help Jim and his team find the answers they needed. Maybe tonight Jim would finally get some much needed rest.

People Change Easily, But Are Difficult To Change

It was Wednesday, and Jim had arrived at his favorite restaurant, Del Frisco's, a few minutes later than he would have liked. He looked around and quickly saw Catherine was already seated and waiting for him in the far corner of the mahogany paneled dining room. Jim and Catherine made small talk for about five minutes before Ken arrived. After exchanging pleasantries and introducing Catherine, Jim decided it was time to get down to business.

"Ken,I hope you had a chance to look at the material I sent over. Where do you think we are going wrong?" Ken had known Jim for a long time and knew Jim appreciated straight talk.

Ken started, "Well, let's begin with a few questions. On the phone you described three major initiatives that you both believe are important to the company's success. Can you explain to me why JenMar is working on each one of them?"

Jim thought for a moment and then answered. "The ITIL initiative is the easiest to answer. Over the last several years JenMar has really struggled with its internal information technology efforts. We have purchased a lot of hardware and software, but time and time again we end up delivering great technical solutions to the wrong business problems behind schedule and over budget. We have some first rate technical people, but we needed to get them focused on delivering real business solutions. The Information Technology Infrastructure Library, or ITIL, is about getting our technical people to focus on the needs of the business in a structured manner."

"I am not familiar with ITIL," Ken stated. "Can you help me understand it a bit better?"

"Sure," Jim continued. "I wasn't that familiar with it either before I got to JenMar, but my CIO is a big proponent so I have been trying to do some reading. ITIL started out as a British government project in the 1980's. The Central Computer and Telecommunications Agency (CCTA) developed a set of standards their research showed were best practices within the information technology industry. The original standards were housed in 42 books that became the IT Infrastructure Library and were built based upon Edward Deming's Plan-Do-Check-Act process model. In the almost three decades since it was originally created, the standards has gone through several revisions and now are contained in the five books of version 3.0. These books include: Service Design, Service Transition, Service Operation, Continual Service Improvement, Service Strategy."

"So ITIL is mostly a government standard?" Ken asked.

"That's what I thought as well when I first heard about it," Jim responded. "But it's not. Although it was originally created by a government organization and is controlled by the UK's Office of Government Commerce, many private organizations also use it. For example, Microsoft used ITIL as the basis in developing their Microsoft Operations Framework (MOF) which we also use at JenMar."

"So how does ITIL get your IT organization for focus on the needs of the business?" Ken asked.

"It took me a little bit to wrap my arms around it, but in a nutshell it focuses everyone's attention on delivering services instead of deploying technology," Jim responded. Jim immediately could tell that Ken was not tracking so he added, "Let me give you an example. When a new employee starts working for us one of the first things they expect is a computer login with e-mail access. They don't care about the hardware or software that is required to deliver those services. They just want their e-mail. ITIL is all about keeping the focus on the things that really matter. In this case, e-mail. Users don't want to hear or care about server problems, software compatibility issues or licenses. They just want it to work."

"OK," Ken said. "I understand, but how does ITIL impact the other major initiatives going on at JenMar?"

"That is a great question," Jim responded. "ITIL includes a project management methodology within its framework. Many people look at this fact and assume you can't do ITIL and establish a PMO together. We don't believe that's true. ITIL is a process model, as I said before. But, it does not dictate who owns the processes, and there is quite a bit of latitude in how ITIL is implemented."

Jim continued. "The program management office development initiative was started so JenMar could become more consistent in its results and so JenMar's senior management could get better visibility on how the different projects were impacting each other across the organization. The PMO owns every new initiative JenMar does, or it provides mentoring to the project leaders in the few cases where they don't own the initiative. The PMO is also responsible for reporting on all new initiatives and it owns the processes and methodologies JenMar uses to complete those initiatives. The processes include the selection of ITIL. The biggest issue for us has been determining the reporting relationships for the PMO."

"So you are saying your PMO isn't just something for the IT organization?" Ken asked.

"I know a lot of organizations look at project management as something that belongs within the IT organization, but I do not." Jim responded. "Poor IT project performance made talking about project management popular, but our organization is like every other. We are only really doing two things, operations, where we are just trying to keep the wheels on the bus turning, or we are doing projects where we are creating the new products and services we need to compete. When I got here JenMar was doing a good job of reporting on its operations, but no one could tell me what was going on with all our projects, and several projects were negatively impacting each other. We desperately needed to get visibility, and that's what I am hoping the PMO will provide. However, for it to work it needs to be more than just IT and it needs to report directly to me.

"Wait a minute," Ken said interrupting Jim. "You just made a big leap that I think is important, and I want to make sure I understand it."

"No problem," Jim replied. "What is it?"

"You said you needed to get visibility to the new initiatives and then immediately jumped to it also needed to report to you. Can you connect the dots for me?"

"I'll try," Jim responded. "I told you about my belief that every organization only does two things operations and projects. Does that make sense?"

"Sure, as a broad generalization I can agree with your statement," Ken responded.

"We have already talked quite a bit about all the cost savings measures my predecessor tried at JenMar, right?"

"Sure," Ken confirmed.

"Those were and are all targeted at improving operations, but they do very little to the way projects are executed," Jim continued. "A lot of organizations try to cut costs on projects, but what usually happens is they simply reduce the number of projects they execute in times of trouble. I believe it is the exact opposite of what we need to do to succeed. You see, I am a contrarian. I believe that down markets are actually incredible opportunities. In a down market it can get pretty darwinistic as economics force a lot of players out of business. To be a survivor you have to be one of the ones taking market share from your competitors. To do that, you have to find a way to introduce new products, services, and efficiencies to the marketplace. That requires us to execute projects better, faster, and cheaper than any of our competitors. For JenMar to execute projects better, faster and cheaper than our competitors everyone in the organization must see project execution being as important as I. Net, I needed to raise the visibility of our projects all the way to the CEO's office. However, even doing that has not solved all our problems implementing the PMO."

"How so?" Ken asked.

"We have really struggled with ownership and politics concerning the PMO. Several members of the executive management team wanted to own it, or wanted to be as far away from owning it as they could. It is one of the reasons I called you."

Ken smiled and replied, "Thanks for the vote of confidence, but before we get into the solutions can you bring your last major initiative into the discussion? I now understand how you are getting ITIL and your PMO efforts to work together, but I am troubled by the Lean Initiative. In my experience, Lean is all about developing a culture of continuous process improvement. Am I correct?"

"Absolutely," Jim confirmed.

"Well, it seems to me that is exactly what you are trying to do with your PMO and ITIL as well. Aren't these initiatives overlapping quite a bit?" Ken asked.

Jim thought for a moment before responding, "Yeah, actually they have. We have tried to prevent the clash by focusing the different initiatives on different groups within the company."

"How has that worked?" Ken asked.

"To be honest, not real well," Jim responded. "We have tried to constrain the Lean Initiative to our operations group, but ITIL's continuous service improvement focus and the PMO's focus on lessons learned has created a lot of confusion as we have tried to push through all these changes."

Ken smiled for a moment and then said, "Jim we have known each other a long time and you have always asked that I be frank with you so I am going to do that today."

Jim smiled too. That was exactly why he liked Ken. He was one of the few consultants he had ever met that did not mince words. "That is exactly what I hoped you would say," Jim affirmed.

Ken continued, "Good. The first thing I have to say is that I have never seen an organization of your size try so many of these initiatives at once. Can you explain why you decided to do them all at once?"

Jim paused as the waiter appeared to deliver their drinks and take their lunch order. Once they had ordered he continued, "Two of the initiatives were already started when I came on board and we started the third because we felt it would be too costly to wait."

Ken then turned to Catherine and asked, "Catherine, in your experience what causes most Lean Initiatives to fail?"

"That's easy," Catherine said. "If the initiate fails it is usually because the organization can't get their people to commit long term to the new way of doing things. They simply fall back into their old habits."

"I have seen that a lot as well," confirmed Ken.

Jim interrupted, "Falling back into old habits is a symptom and not the cause of the problem. What is the root cause?"

Ken looked over to Catherine and asked, "What do you think?"

Catherine responded. "That is an easy one Jim. We talk about it all the time. To succeed everyone in the organization must buy-in to the new ways."

"Well have they bought in?" Ken asked.

 "I thought so," Jim said. "At least until we got the most recent survey results back. Now it seems no one does."

Right then everyone's food arrived so Ken let himself and his two companions take a few bites before he continued, "Jim and Catherine, I think we have found a great place to start to solve JenMar's problems."

Jim finished a bite of his southwestern steak salad and looked at Jim, "I knew you'd be able to help."

Ken finished off his Coke in two quick gulps before answering with a question, "Do either of you know the difference between buy-in and ownership?"

Catherine and Jim looked at each other for a moment quizzically. It was Catherine who responded first,

"Aren't they basically the same thing? It's just a matter of degree."

Jim nodded in agreement, "Yes, that's right."

Ken finished off the last bite of his crab cake sandwich before responding. "No, they're not the same and that is your first problem." Neither Jim nor Catherine had any idea what Ken was talking about. Ken continued, "Let me give you a simple analogy. In the ham and eggs breakfast the chicken is interested and the pig is invested. The chicken gets to lay an egg and walk away, but the pig is not so fortunate." The simple analogy made Jim laugh.

Ken paused to let the idea sink in a little then added, "Being interested is the same as buying-in. Ownership is being invested. If you are successful at only getting buy-in towards you initiatives then as soon as implementing the change gets tough people will stop supporting the change. Buy-in is the same as being sold something. At some point you can easily choose to buy-out. However, if people own the idea, and I mean really believe they had a role in its creation, then they will do whatever it takes to make it work. This is because no one wants to admit their own ideas are wrong."

Ken let this concept sink in for a minute while Jim and Catherine finished their lunches. He then continued. "One of the biggest problems organizations face is the belief by senior management that they can create organizational change by implementing some new process, almost by fiat. It simply does not work that way. Lasting organizational change requires at least the appearance of a bottoms-up approach."

Jim was confused. He had diligently worked to ensure each of JenMar's major initiatives had focus groups and they had used repeated surveys to get input from the employees. He asked all his senior executives to spend time with their teams reviewing each project's goals and objectives. He was pretty sure what they were doing was a bottoms-up approach. Fortunately, Catherine was thinking the same thing and asked Ken to explain further.

Ken continued with a question. "Do you believe the people who work at JenMar change easily?"

Catherine and Jim answered at the same time, "no." Catherine quickly qualified her answer, "JenMar is no different than any other company. People get into habits and once in a habit they do not like to change."

Ken smiled. That was the answer he expected so he then asked, "How many of the JenMar employees would raise their hand at least once if we asked them a few simple questions:

1. Have you ever moved to a new city?
2. Have you ever bought a new house?
3. Have you ever taken a new job?
4. Have you ever gotten married?
5. Have you ever decided to have children?"

Jim and Catherine looked at each other. It was Jim that answered this time, "All of them. So what?"

"Well," said Ken.

"Wouldn't you agree those are all pretty significant life changes?"

"Yes," Jim answered.

"Don't you see?" Ken asked. "Your employees are constantly willing to make massive, life altering changes, yet they are resisting the much less significant changes your management team is trying implement. Why?"

Jim saw where Ken was going and answered, "The difference is ownership. JenMar's employees feel they are making the larger life decisions themselves while our surveys show they feel senior management is making all the decisions on our major initiatives. They have bought in, but they have no ownership."

Catherine quickly added, "Ken, you just described what I have seen at many other companies as well, as soon as even small road blocks are hit people lose interest and the initiative fails, but how can we change it?

Ken looked at his watch, he was going to have to cut the conversation off here or he wouldn't make his next appointment. "I have to get going to another meeting, but why don't we meet first thing Friday morning and

23

we can continue our discussion?" They all agreed to meet at 7:30 AM on Friday morning in Jim's office. As Ken got up to leave he asked Catherine and Jim if they could come up with a few ideas to promote real ownership for the major initiatives at JenMar.

First Define The What Then Define The How

Jim got to the office at 7:00 AM on Friday, just like most days. He liked getting in early because it gave him some quiet time to review e-mail and his calendar for the day while the office was largely empty. No matter how late he seemed to stay each night, there were always 50 new e-mails in his inbox when he got to the office each morning. Today was no exception. After filtering through the 35 or so information-only e-mails, Jim was able to focus on the 15 that required a response. Just before he turned his attention to the suggestions Catherine and he wanted to discuss with Ken to improve the level of ownership within JenMar Jim caught one last e-mail that required a response. Had Jim not been expecting the e-mail he would have totally missed it.

It still really frustrated Jim. Even some of his most senior people struggled to make e-mail an effective tool. Jim was regularly receiving more than 100 e-mails per day, and he was confident that he was no different than most of the people who worked for him. Yet time after time people sent Jim e-mails that were multiple pages in length and they expected Jim to pick out the action they wanted from him buried in the e-mail. Right after sending the response, Jim sent a quick note to his admin concerning e-mail standards. Jim could not remember where he had read it originally, but he found the simple rules concerning e-mail to be worth their weight in gold. As Jim was typing them out he checked his watch. 30 minutes till Ken arrives, plenty of time he thought to himself. He then finished off his rules.

1. E-mail should be used as a confirmation tool and not as a primary means of communication.
2. Don't use e-mail to have *hard* conversations. Talk to people. This means in person whenever possible.
3. Keep e-mails as short as possible. Use bullet points and lots of white space to convey information.
4. Avoid attaching files in e-mails as it leads to all kinds of version management problems. Use collaboration software, hyperlinks, and references to ensure document consistency.
5. If action is expected from the receiver place *ACTION REQUIRED:* in the subject heading along with the requested action. Then explain the request following the rules.
6. For complicated requests, contact the receiver using a second channel of communication to confirm understanding.
7. Do not assume receipt of an e-mail is the same as understanding.
8. Never reply to all when you receive an e-mail that makes you angry or upset. Everyone can tell someone (you or the original sender) is just covering their tail.
9. If you receive an e-mail that is upsetting try sitting on for 24 hours. In many cases you will find that people did not intend for it to be interpreted they

way you did, and a little cooling off will do everyone
good.

Both Ken and Catherine arrived 25 minutes later. Jim
had brought coffee and pastries from Panera's so after
everyone got their coffee and pastry they all sat down
at Jim's office conference table. After a few comments
about the Denver Bronco's chances for the weekend
they got down to work.

Ken began by asking Jim and Catherine what they had
come up with since their lunch two days prior. Jim
suggested Catherine walk Ken through the list.
Catherine was halfway through the list of eight items
when Ken stopped her. Ken asked Catherine and Jim if
any of their ideas aligned to JenMar's strategy.

Jim provided the answer. "If I am doing my job
correctly, everything we do aligns with our strategy."

"Good answer," Ken said. "But does every employee
understand how their work on these particular
initiatives impacts JenMar's strategy?" That question
made Jim sit up in his chair.

"Wait a minute," Jim started. "Are you suggesting our
strategy is defined by the tasks people are doing? I
thought our strategy defined the tasks."

"I would like to say you are absolutely right Jim, but that
is only in theory," Ken responded. "In the real world it
gets complicated. The single most difficult thing for

most organizations to do is establish a strategy and then set and stick to organizational priorities based on that strategy. This means there is only one top priority, one number two, one number three, and so on. It also means the organization must maintain their strategy and priorities, and really make some hard decisions when there is conflict. The tendency is for leaders to want to have lots of top priorities and demand their teams somehow get all the work done. Since there really aren't any defined priorities the workers end up having to make the determination of what they are going to work on first, second, third, and so on. In the real world this is usually done using the squeaky wheel principle. Whoever squeaks the most gets their stuff done first. All of a sudden, the strategy of the senior leadership is meaningless. The real strategy of the organization is being set by the lowest ranking workers based on the order in which they are completing tasks."

When Jim had first taken the job as CEO he had done a quick analysis of the situation and concluded that many of JenMar's problems stemmed from a strategy that did not encompass current market realities and a staff that did not believe in the strategy. Jim and the senior management team had spent significant time reformulating the strategy and then working to open communication with the entire staff. It was obvious to Jim that he had seen the issue but somehow missed something. After a moment, Jim responded, "I am pretty sure I understand, but can you explain further?"

Ken answered with another question, "Jim does JenMar have a process for managing its strategy and other operational efforts?"

"Sure," Jim said. "We formalized a strategic planning process almost as soon as I got here. Our Project Management Office has a process for managing projects. We are using ITIL to manage and improve our IT services. And our continuous process improvement initiative is all about formalizing the improvements throughout the organization. So what?"

"Well," Ken answered. "You have a lot of processes in place, and each of these processes makes a lot of sense to the executive that is championing them, but if your team does not understand the link between these processes and the end goal they will simply perceive the effort as another useless process and they will fail to take ownership." Ken continued, "For the organization to succeed it must make use of the most effective processes and tools towards its desired goals. This is true at both a strategic and an operational or project level. Since no two organizational initiatives are identical the processes organizations use to achieve their objectives will be equally varied. Therefore, you must first define the what, the real deliverable, then define the how, or the methodologies."

Catherine was worried. "Wait a minute," she said "Are you saying the consultants we are using are not adding value?"

"No," Ken responded. "Just the opposite. I am sure there are many consulting firms who do use a cookie-cutter approach with the same basic process for every situation, but most are focused on finding the right solution for their clients' problem."

Jim saw Catherine's concern and wanted to reassure her without losing sight of the point Ken was trying to make. "Catherine, I have every confidence that the consultants you have brought in are doing a great job. So please don't worry. We are both learning here. Ken, if I understand you correctly, we have become too process focused and have lost sight of why we have the processes in the first place. Is that right?"

"Not quite Jim," Ken answered. "In addition to making sure your people understand why you have particular processes, you must also work to ensure your processes are the most effective to achieve the desired goal and provide an organizational prioritization of all initiatives. Let's take your PMO as an example." Ken knew Jim was keenly interested in improving JenMar's delivery of projects from previous discussions.

"OK," Jim responded.

Ken then asked, "Can you tell me what methodology your PMO uses currently?"

"Sure," Jim answered. "When I started here we were largely a waterfall shop, but one of the first problems I noticed was we were struggling to cope with our customers' changing requirements and we often had large time gaps between when we got signoff on the requirements and when we actually delivered the products. We have since changed to a more iterative methodology."

Ken thought he heard something in Jim's tone so he asked, "Jim it doesn't sound like you are completely satisfied with the results from the change. Is that true?"

"Yes," said Jim. "Most of our projects are going more smoothly and our customer satisfaction survey results are up, but about 30% of our projects are actually worse than before."

"That is interesting," Ken responded. "Is there any chance that the under performing projects used to be doing well?"

"Yeah, as a matter of fact they did. Ken, how did you know?"

"Easy really, and Jim I think you already know the answer as well." Ken offered. "Those projects most likely have characteristics that actually work best in a waterfall model. Jim, one of the biggest mistakes organizations consistently make is trying to have a single process or methodology for all their projects.

In most organizations you need at least two or three methodologies for the different types of projects you have, and you need processes in place that guide your project managers through a selection process to find the best methodology for each project."

Catherine was confused and jumped in, "Wait a minute, won't that create chaos and make it impossible to compare results from the different projects?"

"Not at all," Ken answered. "As long as you set up your performance metrics correctly management will not see a difference in reporting, but let's save metrics for our next meeting." Ken looked at his watch briefly. They had been talking for an hour now. "Let me just summarize our conversation. For the organization to achieve its strategy everyone from top to bottom has to take ownership of the strategy. And, for everyone to take ownership of the strategy they must understand how their individual assignments impact the strategy. Additionally, it is critical that the management team selects processes that offer the best opportunity for achieving the desired strategy. Since most organizations have many efforts going on at the same time, success dictates we have several optional processes or methodologies that provide us with the flexibility to meet the situation. Simply put, there is no perfect process."

Jim and Catherine both understood. The key was going to be developing a process that required the organizational leaders to select a methodology as one of their early decisions based on the perceived conditions.

Jim spoke up, "Ken, I think there is more going on here than just a process limitation. Can we talk some more in two weeks?"

"Sure," Ken answered. "How does Friday at the same time in two weeks work for you both? We can talk about Catherine's concern over metrics." Both Jim and Catherine agreed.

After Ken left Catherine and Jim agreed to several steps they could take to make the changes Ken had suggested.

The first time Jim had gotten JenMar's senior management team together to discuss Ken's ideas it had been a rocky start. Everyone had immediately jumped to the same conclusion as Catherine. It took Jim a second and third meeting before everyone on the team really seemed to take ownership of the process issue. Jim decided to separate the issue of setting priorities for now. Jim had been careful to not dictate the conclusion but only provide information and guide the conversation.

Eventually the team had come to the same conclusion Ken had outlined.

Once everyone was on the same page, the team was able to guide the PMO in selecting three methodologies

Waterfall, Spiral, and Scrum to meet the various project needs. The PMO also developed a simple ten item questionnaire to allow the project and product managers to quickly determine the best methodology to successfully complete each initiative. These questions included:

1. How well understood are the project requirements by the business and project stakeholders?
2. Does the project require the use of new technology?
3. If #2 is yes, how well does the team understand the new technology?
4. Does the project require custom development?
5. Does the project involve a high volume transaction system or process?
6. Does the project involve a legacy platform?
7. Does the project involve a thin-client or web technology?
8. Will the project require the use of external consultants?
9. Will the project team have constant access to business stakeholders?
10. What is the experience level of the project team?
11. How large is the project team?

Based upon the insights from JenMar's senior leaders, the PMO had even come to the table with a new project initiation process. The process included a new kickoff meeting and addressed project prioritization. The fact that the PMO was pushing for a prioritization of projects initially surprised Jim. However, the more he thought back to what Ken had said the more it made sense.

It was Wednesday morning and Jim was preparing for a meeting with Chuck Kois, his PMO Director. Jim was excited to get into the details of what Chuck and his team had come up with. "Ten minutes," Jim thought. "Just enough time to finish up."

When Chuck walked into Jim's office Jim could tell he was really proud of his team's work. "Have a seat Chuck over at the conference table, and I be right with you," Jim said as he finished reviewing the last page before walking over to join Chuck.

"Where would you like to start," Chuck asked.

"I want to make sure I fully understand what your team is proposing. So let's start at the beginning and go through everything you've got," Jim replied.

"OK," Chuck replied. "I think we can get through everything in the hour we have. But, to be sure I will go quickly and just ask you to stop me if you have questions."

"I always do, don't I?" Jim said laughing.

"Absolutely," Chuck replied. "OK. Here goes. We are suggesting everything begins with the submission of a project request form. The form is to be submitted to the PMO by whomever wants the work done and will cover everything outside of operational issues or maintenance fixes."

"That sounds like this is for IT only. Did I miss something?" Jim asked.

"No," Chuck replied. "It's for all groups. Sorry it wasn't clear."

"No problem," Jim replied. "So what would form look like?"

"We are keeping the form easy, I learned a long time ago that the more complicated you make the form the less likely people are to use it. I know there are a ton of questions we might ask, but we stuck to a half page form with four basic questions." Chuck handed Jim a copy of the PMO's project request form.

Requestor: _____ Date: _____
Required Delivery Date: _____
Business Need: _____
_____
_____
Why is it needed: _____
_____
_____

The simplicity of the form surprised Jim, but he was also pleased. "So, I complete this form then what happens?" he asked.

"The next step in the process is the PMO will take the request and determine the answers to the following questions:

1. Is the request feasible?
2. What resources would likely be required to complete the project?
3. Roughly how long would it take to complete the project?
4. Does the project link in some way to an already approved project and if so what would be the impacts of adding this one?

All of the answers to these questions are assumed to be Rough Order of Magnitude, or ROM estimates. This means everyone would have to understand they were +/- 50%." Chuck stated.

"OK. Now I am confused," Jim said. "How could you ever hope to answer these questions with only a half page form completed, and why is there such a large variance? Won't the lack of information make it impossible to create accurate budgets?"

"The issue is actually the exact opposite," Chuck replied. "As the team and I have worked through the issues of setting up the PMO we found a big problem."

"What was that?" Jim asked.

"We have never even attempted to track how much time or money we spend planning our projects," Chuck replied.

"Why is that a big problem?" Jim asked carefully not sure he was ready for the answer. Then adding quickly adding before Chuck could respond, "What's wrong with simply making the planning process part of the general administration expectations?"

"The problem surfaces in two areas," Chuck answered. "First, we have no idea how much time we are spending to do the planning work. You might initially think that is no big deal because it is just a cost of doing business, but the truth is different sizes and types of projects take differing amounts of time to plan. Like most organizations, none of our people are working on only one thing at a time. We are all working on a mixture of approved projects, potential projects and operational responsibilities. By not tracking the time spent planning the initiative we have no idea how much more we can handle, whether we are correctly staffed, or where we are the most resource constrained. We are always receiving an incomplete management picture."

"I am not sure I agree with you," Jim responded. "I am not sure I believe project planning really takes up that much time. Also, this does not address the issue of the large variances in the budget estimates. Help me see what I am missing."

"It is not what you are missing," Chuck responded, "It is what you can't prove. The truth is neither of us knows what is really happening. As a result we don't know if we are missing a big piece of the puzzle or a minor one. Without this information we can never get accurate estimates. Considering all the trouble we have had delivering projects in the past, the team and I felt it was time to figure it out. We simply can't afford to not know."

"OK," Jim said. "Sounds like you are telling me we need to start collecting the data so we can know what we don't know. What is your second area you mentioned?"

"The area of concern is that by not tracking the planning efforts it makes most of our project staff look incredibly inefficient. A big piece of their job is building, monitoring and maintaining project plans inclusive of their schedules. That time is not free, but we treat it like it is."

"OK," Jim started. "Say I buy your argument, what does not tracking our project have to do with our discussion about the questions you want to ask?"

"I know it seems like a side issue, but the reason I mentioned these two problems is that we have mostly assumed this stuff is either a big black hole that we can't answer so why try, or we have assumed we need to get every question answered up front. For example, many of our project managers believe they must get all the scope and requirements defined at the very beginning before moving ahead with a project. We are recommending a third option. We want everyone to understand we have imperfect information. We will use a well designed, strategically focused process to capture information as soon as it is practically possible. In other words, it is impossible to get all the requirements and details up front so let's focus on what we can know and use data to track and improve our performance over time."

"If I understand you correctly, you are suggesting we get our people to trust each other and our process to gather information. Then capture how long it actually takes to plan each project so we can include that time and money in the determination of project budgets and schedules. Over time we should gain improved accuracy which will help us manage our portfolio as well as future projects. Is that correct?" Jim concluded.

"Absolutely!" Chuck enthusiastically responded.

"Seems reasonable," said Jim. "So what happens once the PMO has answered your four questions?"

"The PMO will then evaluate the answers and use a basic scoring model to create a value for each proposed project. The score along with the other project information will then be presented to the governance committee for a decision." Chuck responded.

"Can you explain more about this score you are recommending?" Jim asked.

"What we have come up with so far is pretty basic," Chuck answered. "We used Microsoft Excel to create a form with ten categories or questions. Each category is evaluated on a Likert Scale using a drop-down menu for each row. The categories include:

1. Level of sponsorship support (willingness to commit resources & money)
2. Unfamiliarity with technical solution or outside the current enterprise architecture
3. New or significantly changed business process(es)
4. Funding source complexity (where is the money coming from)
5. Stakeholder complexity (involvement with groups & individuals outside the organization)
6. JenMar internal stakeholder complexity
7. Financial risk tied to not undertaking project
8. Level of customer/user support (non-sponsor)
9. Resources complexity (involvement with contractors, subcontractors, etc.)
10. Project restart - Recovery from a previously failed project

For each category a PMO representative selects one of five choices: Very High, High, Neutral, Low or Very Low."

"But, how is the score calculated?" Jim asked.

"Each question has a maximum value of 100. If the category answer is Very High the category score is 100. If the category answer is High the score is 80. If the answer is Neutral the score is 60. If the answer is Low the score is 40, and if the answer is Very Low the score is 20." Chuck explained. "The scores are then added together to derive the overall project score. This value along with the other collected data is then provided to the Portfolio Governance Board. We are recommending we use you and your direct reports as the Portfolio Governance Board," Chuck concluded.

"What would be the responsibilities of this governance board?" Jim asked.

"The Portfolio Governance Board would make all project approval decisions and would receive regular performance reports," Chuck responded.

"I am not sure we could support that. It sounds like you are putting an extra burden on the senior staff that really should be handled at a lower level." Jim said hesitantly. "Tell me more."

Chuck hesitated for a moment fearing he had just lost Jim's support then began. "This issue the team saw was a need to get senior management input on our priorities and provide input the PMO might not have about where the organization was going. Unfortunately, politics plays too much of a role in many resource decisions today. We believe this largely occurs because we lack this information and are often left to fill in the gaps."

This was starting to sound an awful lot like the conversation Jim had with Ken, Jim thought before asking, "But how would this work without completely over-burdening the senior staff?"

Chuck saw Jim's concern and was confident he had the answer. "We are asking the Portfolio Governance Board to meet once every other week for 45 minutes. At least 72 hours prior to each meeting the members of the Board will be provided with an executive summary of the status on all current projects and all new requests. The key will be maintaining the set times for each discussion. The only work for the Board members will be to review the reports and participate in the meetings." Chuck paused for a moment then added, "And, they must be willing to stick with the decisions they collectively make."

Jim thought through what Chuck was proposing. It made sense and aligned with what he had discussed from Ken. He knew it would be a tough sell with his leadership team, especially the sticking to the team's decision, but it was the right choice. "OK, Chuck you have a go ahead to bring it all together and hold the first governance meeting. I believe you and the PMO are going to make a big difference for JenMar," Jim concluded.

Chuck took his cue and thanked Jim for his time and headed back to his office to tell the PMO team the good news. They were going to be very busy.

Manage Deliverables Not Tasks

Jim and Catherine were both glad Friday was now here. It had been two weeks since their last meeting with Ken. In that time they had made significant progress with the senior management team. As Jim and Catherine sat waiting for Ken to arrive they discussed the progress they had made and several ideas they each had for improvements. When Ken finally arrived ten minutes later he found Catherine and Jim in a heated debate over one of the current projects. "Sorry for being late," Ken said as he sat down.

"No problem," said Jim. "It gave us a chance to review the early results for our new methodology process and we have run into a problem with which you might be able to help."

"Sure. Why don't you tell me what is happening," Ken suggested.

"Well, I have to qualify our situation," Jim started. "I think we are a little unusual as an organization because I do not think most companies have the CEO involved in the development of methodology and process the way I have been."

Ken offered his agreement before Jim continued.

"Because of my involvement, I believe it has been easier for JenMar to move these changes ahead. I also think we have done pretty good job of staying on track, although I am a little concerned about the long-term ability of maintaining the initiatives. But, I think we have a real problem." Jim paused for a moment before continuing.

In a reversal of roles it was Ken who asked, "What do you mean?"

Jim leaned forward in his chair and said, "Everyone seems to be supportive of the changes we have made, but we do not seem to be seeing any significant improvements in the performance of our major initiatives and I just do not understand why. Ken, I am beginning to question the things we are doing that I know are right. What am I missing?"

Ken looked at Jim and Catherine for a moment and appeared worried. After a few seconds, he finally asked Jim, "Can you be more specific?"

"Sure," Jim said. "We are using the things you taught us, but we are not seeing the actual delivery of business results improve. Ken, you have done a lot of work for me over the years and you have always come through for me, but frankly right now I am nervous. We have worked very hard to get JenMar's people to take ownership of the initiatives. We have worked hard at ensuring the teams clearly understand the scope of the initiative, but we are still not seeing significant improvement in the business results. My portfolio dashboards still seem to show every project as being on time until the last possible moment when suddenly they are not."

Jim's last statement did not make any sense to Ken so he asked, "Jim, what do you mean suddenly they are not?"

"Just what I said," Jim responded. "Most of our projects report out they are on schedule till very late in the process, and yet almost every time we miss the targeted delivery date by a wide margin. I know our teams are working hard, no one is intentionally reporting false information, and unforeseeable things do happen, but on nearly every project?"

Ken thought for a moment and then said, "It sounds like you are left with one of two conclusions Jim: either your people are incompetent or something else is going on. Which option do you hope it is?"

"Not much of a choice there," Jim responded. "Like every other leader, I believe our people are pretty good."

Ken smiled, "You are in luck, or at least I think so. There are several things that cause projects to be delayed.

Unfortunately, very few of those things have to do with a technology, modeling, or a mathematical technique.

The causes of delays almost always have to do with people, which make them a lot harder to solve. When we talk about project delays the most frequent causes are:

1. Unfocused project management
2. A focus on task management
3. Not managing to probability
4. Parkinson's Law
5. Mismanagement of safety
6. A lack of performance metrics
7. Multi-tasking

Unfocused project management simply means we ask our project managers to manage more than one initiative at a time. In many cases this is a necessary reality. However, it is critical that senior leaders watch that we are not over allocating our resources. A good rule of thumb is to never assign a resource that can give less than 20% of their time. The second issue, task management, is the one I'd like to discuss today if that is alright with you."

"Sure," responded Jim.

"When do you get value from the efforts of your resources?" Ken asked.

"We get value when the resources actually delivery the business result," Jim stated.

Ken then asked, "Do you get any value when the deliverable is only partially complete?"

"Sometimes, but that usually only happens as an exception or when we settle for less than the complete result," Jim answered.

"So do you get any value from the fact that your resources are working hard?" Ken asked.

"Not really," Jim answered.

"So why do all of your project managers report where the resources are on their tasks?" Ken asked.

Jim thought for a moment, and then said, "I don't think I understand where you are going."

Ken picked up one of the status reports sitting on the table, and asked Jim and Catherine, "Is this a typical JenMar status report?"

"Yes, that is our standard template," Jim answered.

"What is the standard metric you use for performance?" Ken asked.

"It's right here," Jim said pointing to a value at the top of the report. "It is the percent complete."

"Let me make an analogy," Ken suggested. "Imagine you are a track coach, and it is your job to coach the U.S. men's 4 x 100 meter relay team in the Olympic

Games. Each one of your runners is considered one of the ten fastest men in the world and no other team has more than two of the top ten runners. Do you like your odds?"

"Definitely," Jim responded.

"Well, Jim that is exactly what the situation was for the last Olympics, yet not only did the U.S. not win, the U.S. did not even make it out of the qualifying heats. Do you remember why?"

"Sure," Jim responded. "The U.S. team dropped the baton and was disqualified."

"Right," Ken said. "Winning a relay race means being the first team to get the baton across the finish line. In this case would the results have been any different if you had told the middle two runners they needed to run their legs faster?"

"Of course not," Jim answered. "The baton would still be dropped, and they still would have been disqualified."

"Exactly," Ken suggested. "It is the same as managing tasks in projects. When the focus is on managing tasks it is possible for resources to be working incredibly hard and not delivering any value. The only way to prevent this problem is for senior management to hold project managers accountable to delivering real business results. Therefore, when asking questions about status the focus must be on the deliverables not tasks. Asking for percent complete is focusing project managers on tasks and not on deliverables."

"Wow," Jim said after a moment of silence. "I had never thought about it that way, but it makes sense. Today, we hold everyone accountable to how hard they are working and almost every project manager reports they are right on track until the very end of the project when suddenly at the last minute we go into crisis mode to deliver the project. And, it happens over and over again. In many cases, we end up extending the delivery date or de-scoping the initiative." But, how can we solve the problem?" Jim asked.

"There are several things causing this problem Jim," Ken answered. "But, the first step is to have an honest assessment of where the initiatives are really. To do this have your project managers get the answers to two questions: How many hours have been spent on the deliverable and secondly, how many hours are left."

"What difference will those questions make?" Jim asked. "Isn't that just adding a calculation the problem, and won't our resources just inflate or artificially adjust the numbers?" he quickly added.

"If your project managers allow themselves to collect information they know to be blatantly false it will not improve anything," Ken responded. "However, here is the first advantage of this process. Imagine you are a team leader who has just had their boss require them to collect this information. Now imagine you have some resource who is assigned to a deliverable that originally was estimated to take 40 hours. In the first weekly status meeting this resource reports that they spent 30 hours of their time working on the deliverable and they believed they have 30 hours left. Assuming this resource was the only one assigned to the deliverable what do you now know?"

"I know that the resource believes they are halfway done with the deliverable, and that they believe it is going to take 50% longer than originally estimated," Jim answer.

"Perfect." Ken replied. "Now imagine at the end of the second week that same resource comes into the status meeting and again reports that they spent 30 hours on the deliverable and they believe that they have 30 hours left. What would you think?" Ken asked.

"Well," Jim replied. "They are now telling me that it is going to take 90 hours to complete a 40 hour deliverable, and it sounds a little fishy that the numbers are identical from one week to the next. I would want a real good explanation."

"That is exactly right." Ken said. "Do see how the reporting requirements provide greater visibility to what is happening?"

"I think it makes sense, but isn't this a little low level for me as the CEO of the organization?" Jim asked.

"In a few cases I would say yes. However, I have learned over the years that senior executives only get the information they need when it is collected at the right level of granularity beneath them. Most organizations do not do this well and rarely is there any consistency. Therefore, it's critical that you set up the right demands on your people if you are going to be able to make the top level changes you need to make. Does that make sense?"

"I am still a little concerned that we are not at the right level, but I will trust you Ken." Jim replied.

"How about I give you a couple of weeks so you can have your team put together the answers and then we can talk about where to go next?" Ken suggested.

"Sounds good," Jim responded. "Same time in two weeks?"

"Sure," Ken answered as the two friends shook hands and then Ken left Jim and Catherine to get to work.

Over the next two weeks Jim and Catherine focused on making the changes Ken had suggested. Jim had asked Catherine to work with JenMar's project managers to collect the needed data. Almost immediately the project managers resisted the request. To the project managers the request for reporting on deliverables was no different than what they had always been doing, and Catherine was struggling to see the difference as well. After all, what is the difference between building a component and the component itself she thought to herself? However, Jim thought it was important, so she worked hard to get the numbers. What she found surprised her.

When she and Jim began reviewing the results it appeared JenMar was doing very well which did not make sense. After all, the entire reason for working with Ken had been the fact that the company was not delivering business results. She and Jim had then tried to sort and group the initiatives using just about every technique they could think of and none of it made any sense. That is, until they sorted the projects by lifecycle. Then it hit them like a brick.

Just as Ken had predicted, almost every project was reporting on time and on budget performance until very late in the process when almost universally they all became late and/or over budget. Many were de-scoped or new phases were required to complete the desired results. It seemed JenMar's projects never ended they just entered a new phase.

Once they had showed this trend to all the managers, most willingly began trying the new reporting methodology. It had only been two weeks so they did not have any real results from the change, but at least they better understood the problem.

Manage Starts Not Finishes

As Ken parked his brand new Cadillac Escalade Hybrid he thought to himself how good consulting had been to him and his family. Over the last several years he had been able to carve out a nice niche market working with companies like JenMar. Yet, he was always surprised by the need for what he did. As he opened the door to JenMar he thought, "All I teach is common sense. It is just amazing how uncommon it really is, even with gifted executives."

Jim and Catherine were seated and waiting for Ken when he walked into Jim's office. After exchanging brief pleasantries Jim got everyone down to business by having Catherine explain what they had found and the actions they had taken. After she finished Jim asked, "We haven't seen any results in only two weeks, but what do you think?"

Ken took a moment or two to look over the reports and then said, "I know it might not seem like it, but you have taken a major step forward. Any real advancement requires you to know where you really are. The data you are now collecting will allow you to make that determination. The next step is to change the way you manage your people."

When Jim heard this he shut his eyes and half muttered, "That sounds painful..."

"Unfortunately, for many organizations," Ken responded, "It is the most painful and difficult part of the process. Worse, if you don't do it you will never see significant improvement in the delivery of your initiatives."

"Alright," Jim sighed, "I guess you better explain what you mean then."

Ken smiled and started, "It won't be quite that bad Jim, but what makes the next step so difficult is that it involves a major culture shift. As we discussed earlier, change is hard and it requires the leadership to get the entire organization to take ownership of the required shift."

"I remember," Jim responded. "And, I really believe that is true. We have seen it work here at JenMar."

"I am glad to hear that," Ken said before continuing. "Let me begin with an analogy. Jim, I know you have two kids, but Catherine, do you have any children?"

"Yes, I have three," Catherine responded proudly. "They are fourteen, eleven, and eight."

"Great," Ken responded. "What is the first thing you both tell your children they must do when they come home from school?"

Catherine and Jim looked at each other for a moment quizzically for a moment before answering in unison, "Homework and their chores."

Next Ken asked them both, "Why do you ask them to complete their homework and chores before they play?"

Ken had to laugh a little before continuing. He knew Jim's eldest son Kevin well. He was the starting quarterback at his high school and all he ever seemed to think about were girls and football, not necessarily in that order. "Jim, I'll bet Catherine's kids are exactly the same." Catherine nodded in agreement before Ken went on, "In fact, every time I have used this analogy people answer just like you did. It seems every parent has learned the same life lesson you both have. When it comes to your children, they have to start with the hard stuff that they do not want to do first otherwise it will not get done. There are two questions you both should be asking yourselves at this point."

Neither Jim nor Catherine had any idea what those questions might be, and Ken could tell. After letting them think for a moment Ken added, "The first question you should be asking is why? Why is it that the vast majority of parents require their children to do their homework and chores first?" Then Ken stopped and gave Catherine and Jim a chance to think about the question, but it didn't take that long.

After only a few seconds Catherine spoke, "Most of us know that if our kids don't get the work done first it will either be very late at night before it gets done or it won't get done at all."

Ken turned to Jim, "Do you agree with that answer?"

"Sure," Jim responded.

"OK," Ken continued. "Let's put what you just told me into '*management speak*' and see if it makes sense. If resources do not get the hardest work out of the way first they likely will miss their deadlines or will not get it done at all. The reason this will happen is because the resources use up all their safety at the beginning of the deliverable and therefore have no safety to fall back on if everything does not go perfectly. How often have either of you ever had everything go perfectly?"

Both Jim and Catherine responded "not very often."

Then Jim asked, "I want to make sure I am using the same definition of safety as you."

"Safety represents time in the estimate that is above the actual number of hours, days, or weeks required to do the work," Ken answered.

After confirming Jim understood Ken continued, "So when the deliverable gets delayed because things did not go as planned and there is no safety to fall back on there is no choice, you must either add costs in terms of overtime or more resources, delay the delivery date or reduce the scope. Does that make sense to both of you?"

"Sure," Catherine and Jim responded.

"So here is the second question." Ken paused for a moment which caused both Jim and Catherine to lean in a little. "If this is true at home, what makes either you think the situation is any different at work?"

This time it was Jim who answered. "Wait a minute.

Neither of us ever said anything of the sort."

"Sure you did, Jim. In fact, you do it every day," Ken said. "Every day you go come in to the office and ask your resources to work on multiple projects at the same time and hold them accountable to the finish dates. The natural outcome is they work on the crisis-of-the-day. Whichever manager screams the loudest has their initiative worked on first. Project managers plan their project based on the desired finish dates and constantly work to add more and more safety to estimates.

Operational managers are requiring the basic operations be maintained. Yet, no matter how much safety they add, and I promise you that almost every deliverable on every initiative has at least 50% safety built into the estimate, everyone keeps struggling to meet their delivery date."

When Ken had finished Jim got up from the conference table and walked over to the window. It was a beautiful day, and Jim would have much preferred to be out on the golf course, especially now. He was pretty sure he understood what Ken was talking about, but he didn't understand how to fix the problem. After a minute or so Jim turned around and looked at his team.

"OK. Let's say I believe what you are saying and I agree that all of us have been incredibly hypocritical in the way we manage our kids versus work resources. How can we begin to be consistent? The same rules just don't apply." When Jim had finished he sat back down and waited for Ken's answer. He didn't have to wait long.

"Can we agree that the real result we are all after is predictably delivery real business results, and that JenMar is not doing so well in that department right now?" Ken asked. Both Catherine and Jim nodded in agreement before Ken continued. "Part of our predictability goal is finishing on time and unfortunately, this is counter intuitive. Almost every manager attempts to hold their people to finish dates, but what do you suppose would happen if you held your resources accountable to when they started working on the deliverable and their level of effort?"

At this point Catherine jumped in, "We couldn't do that! It would be a disaster!"

"Why Catherine?" Ken asked.

"We would miss every deadline and never deliver anything," Catherine responded.

Half under his breath Jim said, "How is that any different than what is happening now?" Then he added with more confidence, "Ken at this point I am ready to try anything. How do we make this work?"

Ken asked if he could use Jim's dry erase board. Jim quickly nodded, and as Ken picked up the blue marker to write out the steps he began, "You need to do a few things:

Continue to provide managers and resource with the due dates, but make sure these are referred to as deadlines and not hard dates.

Manage each resource by holding them accountable for their start date and how hard they work on each deliverable.

Create organizational priorities that do not constantly change, and make hard decisions based on those priorities.

Have real consequences when people do not start their work on time.

These four steps will be some of the hardest changes you have had to make Jim." Ken concluded, "Remember, this is about culture change and you need your people to take ownership." Ken put the lid on the dry erase marker and sat down.

Jim then turned to Catherine for confirmation and said, "Ken, I think we both understand. Although we have a lot of work to do and it will take time, I am confident our people can make this change. We have to. If JenMar is going to survive we have to become known as a company that can deliver what we promise when we promise it, and we have to be able to accomplish these results without killing our people."

For the first time since Ken had been working with

JenMar they did not set a follow up meeting. They all agreed it was time for a break and they would get back together when they had enough data to move onto the next step.

Performance Metrics

It had been a month since Ken had heard from JenMar. He was starting to get concerned. So the previous Friday he had sent Jim an e-mail just to check in. Just as always Jim had responded promptly. It seemed Jim was never without his Blackberry. He assured Ken that they were making progress. Also, Jim suggested they get together the following week.

Ken arrived in Jim's office ten minutes after Catherine. After a few brief moment of small talk Ken asked for an update. Jim let Catherine provide the update. When she had finished Ken smiled. "It sounds like you have begun making some real headway," he said.

"I think we have," Jim responded. The expression on Ken's face however made both Jim and Catherine very nervous. Jim tried to be patient, but he knew he was waiting for the other shoe to drop.

After only about 15 seconds Catherine jumped in, "What did we miss?"

Ken answered with a pair of simple questions. "You both seem to feel that things are really moving in the right direction correct?"

"Absolutely!" they both responded in unison.

"Well," Ken asked. "How do you know?"

This was the part of Ken Jim sometimes hated. Ken had this amazing way of not only being right, but always having one more thing that you had missed. What made it worse was the fact that he was so nice about it. "Can you be more specific?" Jim asked.

"I mean, how do you know the changes you are making are really working," Ken responded. "Think about it Jim, before the latest survey you were pretty confident in the progress of the Lean Initiative as well. So how do you know that JenMar is achieving the desired results?"

Jim and Catherine both looked at each other and thought. After a couple of seconds Catherine finally answered, "I guess we don't."

"Don't get too down guys," Ken offered. "You aren't any different than most leaders. Most executives think everything is going well until it isn't. Unfortunately, by then it's usually too late. The things you are doing now involve a lot of changes for your people and many of them are probably not very comfortable right now," Ken said. "If you want any change or even a project to be successful you must reinforce the desired behaviors with metrics." Ken was concerned that he had lost both of them. It was time to try a different tactic.

"Jim, as you know I spend most of my time speaking to senior leaders just like yourself, and after almost 20 years I can tell what is truly important to them based on just two things. The first of these two things is how they measure their people."

Jim thought he understood where Ken was going, but asked "can you explain some more?"

"Sure," offered Ken. "There is an old adage that says, if you tell me how you are going to measure me I will tell you how I am going to perform. What this is suggesting is that people will adjust their behavior to achieve high marks on whatever metric is used to evaluate them. This point is especially impactful if you have no quantitative metrics," Ken said. Then it hit Jim. Ken was talking about JenMar. Most of the evaluations done by the JenMar team were surveys and individual managers' assessments. They didn't really have any quantitative metrics used across the organization.

Ken let it sink in for a minute before he continued. "Think about the performance you are seeing on your major initiatives today. Is it inconsistent at best with some people doing very well, some people doing poorly and most of your staff in the middle?"

"Sure it is, "Jim answered, "but that is the way it is with every company. It's just the law of averages. Not every employee can be a top performer."

"That's a pretty dangerous notion for JenMar isn't it?" Ken asked. "I mean if a majority of JenMar's staff is just middle-of-the-road and some are even poor aren't you at best just a mediocre company?" Jim had never thought about it that way, but Ken was making sense. Ken continued, "The reason most organizations evaluate their people on a curve, with a few rating high, a few rating low and most people in the middle is because the human resources department demands it be done that way out of a fear that managers won't want to rate poor employees as poor." If JenMar's staff really had the normal distribution then they would probably never produce the best products.

Jim thought for a moment and then suggested, "I don't think that is what I meant. I do believe we have a great work force. Our people are better than anyone else's in our industry."

Ken stopped Jim there. "Again, I have to ask, how do you know?" Ken was silent for several minutes letting both Catherine and Jim ponder what Ken was asking. Finally, Ken broke the silence. "This is one of the most important factors in any organization's success, and it doesn't matter whether we are talking about change issues or achieving your strategy. You must establish quantitative metrics that if met lead to the desired results." Ken added, "If completion of the metrics does not lead to the desired results you do not have the right metrics. And remember, your resources will adjust their behavior to achieve the desired metrics if they know you are really going to hold them accountable."

Jim now understood. He looked over at Catherine and said, "Ken's right, we have some work to do." Then turning to Ken he asked, "Can we meet in another four weeks at the same time?"

"Sure," Ken answered. "But, before I go I want to give you a head start." Ken reached into his briefcase and pulled out a single piece of paper that was letter sized. Ken handed the paper to Jim and said, "I know our focus today was on staff management, but I want to give this to you anyway. This is a PDS, or a Project Datasheet. I know it only covers projects, but I think it can help you. It is filled out with a sample project to help understand how it works."

Jim took the PDS and looked at it. What he saw was an 8.5" x 11" sheet of paper split down the middle at about 20 percent from the top. The top 20 percent contained three arrows: scope, cost, and schedule. One arrow was pointed up. Ken explained this represented a metric that had gotten better since the last reporting period. Another arrow was pointed sideways. Ken explained this represented a stable metric since the last reporting period. The final arrow was pointing downward. This, Ken explained represented a metric that had gotten worse since the last reporting period. To the right of the arrows were a series of acronyms: CV, SV, EAC, CPI, SPI and Sch. Est. Jim had no idea what these meant.

Jim asked, "What are the abbreviations about that appear underneath the Status Date field?"

"They represent key Earned Value statistics," Ken responded. "They provide a quantitatively based method of measuring performance. The key statistics are the CPI and SPI. With both, you are looking for a value of one which means you are on schedule and budget. A value of less than one indicates you are either over budget, with CPI, or behind schedule with the SPI. A value over one indicated you are ahead of schedule and/or under budget."

Ken paused for a moment to let Jim and Catherine catch up before continuing. "A CPI of 0.89 indicates you are 11% over budget. Whereas, an SPI of 1.06 indicates you are 6% ahead of schedule. Using these Earned Value statistics you can calculate the likely actual total project costs and the likely completion date which are represented by the EAC, or Estimate At Completion, and the Sch. Est., or Schedule Estimate. The arrows are measured against these numbers as well. A green arrow represents a less than 10% variance. A yellow arrow represents a variance between 10% and 20%, and a red arrow represents a variance greater than 20%."

"That makes sense," Jim commented. "And, I understand the lines beneath those values, but what are the checkboxes for?"

"There are three sets of checkboxes beneath the indicators. The first set is for the development methodology being used on the project," Ken said. "As we have already discussed, there is no perfect methodology, and each methodology has different requirements and expectations. To ensure everyone is one the same page, it is important that the methodology to be used is clearly communicated. The first checkbox provides a constant reminder of how the project is being run. The second checkbox tells everyone whether or not they should expect to see values in the earned value boxes."

"What about the last checkboxes?" Catherine asked. "What is stage gate management?"

"Stage gate management is a tool designed to make it easier to stop bad projects," Ken responded. He could immediately tell he had misspoken. The term *bad* had likely made both Jim and Catherine uncomfortable so he quickly continued.

"Let me explain what I mean. We have all seen projects that no longer fit with the organizational strategy, or should not be continued because technologies or business needs change. In a traditional management process it is very difficult to cancel unwanted projects because someone likely used political capital to get the project started in the first place. Rarely does anyone want to admit they wasted their efforts. The result is that these projects are allowed to continue indefinitely. Stage gate management reverses this trend by setting a series of gates or milestones throughout the project. Each time a milestone or gate is reached the project sponsor has to sign off that the team has delivered what was promised and that the sponsor wants the work to continue. If for any reason the sponsor does not want the project to continue all they have to do is nothing. If however they sign off it becomes very difficult for them to claim the team failed to deliver or they did not want the project to continue."

"Makes sense," said Jim. "But, what about the chart and the other boxes?"

"The chart represents the trends for each of the three variables scope, schedule and cost that are also represented by the arrows at the top of the page," Ken answered. "The other boxes tell you:

1. The major project stakeholders
2. The project scope statement
3. The project success criteria in a quantitative, tangible way.
4. Any extra key performance indicators
5. The key constraints and assumptions for the project
6. Prioritization of the project management triple constraints with schedule and budget targets
7. The project alignment with the business strategy
8. Project risks and milestones or phases
9. Both the change management and communication management plan

The spaces are small and designed for a 10 point font so you have to be brief, but you are not trying to provide every piece of information about the project. You are just trying to provide the basic rules you intent to use to run the project and a synopsis of the current status on a single sheet of paper," Ken concluded.

Both Jim and Catherine understood. The PDS was going to be a powerful tool to improve communication and performance for JenMar.

"This is great!" Jim commented. "I am really glad you brought this in. It is going to be a key part of our PMO. I am going to get it to the head of our PMO immediately. You wouldn't happen to have an electronic version we could use and a rights release?" Jim asked.

"No problem, I can e-mail it to you this afternoon. In terms of rights, I have not copyrighted it so people could actually use it. And to tell the truth, I didn't invent it. I found a version of it in Jim Highsmith's book <u>Agile</u> <u>Project</u> <u>Management</u> and significantly modified it so it would work for all projects." Ken answered.

Jim checked his watch. They were already over their allotted time by ten minutes. He needed to get going or he would be late to his next meeting. Jim thanked Ken and concluded the meeting. They all shook hands and Ken left Jim and Catherine to start working.

Performance Metrics

		Status Date:				
Scope:	CV:		CPI:			
Schedule:	SV:		SPI:			
Cost:	EAC:		Sch. Est:			

Project Datasheet

Project Name:		Project Manager:	
Project Start Date:		Product Manager:	
Project Budget Est.:		Executive Sponsor:	

Development Methodology: ☐ Waterfall ☐ Spiral ☐ Agile   Earned Value Reporting: ☐ Yes ☐ No   Stage Gate Mgmt: ☐ Yes ☐ No

Primary Stakeholders:	Performance Trends

Legend: Actual Costs — Actual Results — Budget

Project Scope Statement	Project Success Criteria

Project Key Performance Indicators (KPIs)	Key Constraints / Assumptions

Pyramid Management

	Fixed	Flexible	Accept	Priority
Scope	☐	☐	☐	
Quality	☐	☐	☐	
Schedule	☐	☐	☐	
Costs	☐	☐	☐	

Baseline Duration: _____   Actual Costs: _____
Project Prioritization (# out of # for org.): _____

Project Justification

Business Benefit

Increased Revenue	☐
Operational Efficiency	☐
Reduced Costs	☐
Regulatory / Mandate	☐

Portfolio Fit

Tranform	☐
Grow	☐
Run	☐

Major Project Milestones and/or Phases	Primary Risks

Change Management Process	Communication & Reporting Process

Sponsor Approval:		Date:	
PM Approval:		Date:	

Ken's Sample PDS

Late, Over Budget Technical Successes Are Failures

As Ken drove to JenMar's headquarters in the Denver Technology Center he passed the time listening to the local sports talk radio station analyze yet another Broncos' defeat. "Where had the glory days gone?" he thought to himself. It had been a month since Ken had met with Jim and Catherine and he was interested to see their results. Jim's assistant met him at the door and escorted Ken through security and straight into Jim's office where Jim and Catherine were already waiting with more than a dozen color charts, graphs and tables spread out on Jim's conference table.

As Ken and Catherine settled into their seats Jim started the meeting. "Ken, we took your advice to heart and have spent the last month really digging into the metrics we use to evaluate our performance. Catherine and I both agree the metrics we are using give a fair representation of how well JenMar is doing, but we wanted to walk you through what we found."

"Great," Ken said. "Where do you want to start?"

Jim looked over the different reports and selected one that was in the middle of the table. "Let's start here. This is our portfolio dashboard. It shows the current status of each of our major projects. It also shows the budget and delivery date for each initiative." Jim handed Ken the report and gave Ken a moment to review the document.

Project	Scope Status	Schedule Status	Cost Status	Work Status	Original Budget	Actual Cost	Cost EAC	Original Schedule	Schedule EAC
Super System Development	↑	↔	↑	85%	$ 2,600,000	$ 3,700,000	$ 4,342,361	16 Weeks	16.25 Weeks
Hong Kong Order Entry Project	↔	↔	↓	52%	$ 650,000	$ 375,000	375,000	12 Weeks	12 Weeks
New Website Project	↑	↑	↑	56%	150,000	96,000		4 Weeks	6 Weeks
Dubai Production Control Project	↑	↑	↑	44%	2,675,000	1,245,700	2,308,750	32 Weeks	31 Weeks
Ohio Inventory Project	↓	↓	↓	57%	560,000	400,000	700,000	9 Weeks	11 Weeks
CRM Project	↑	↑	↓	43%	680,000	320,000	741,250	12 Weeks	12 Weeks
Portfolio Management Project	↓	↑	↔	27%	400,000	125,000		16 Weeks	21 Weeks
ERP Project Phase II	↔	↑	↑	33%	1,250,000	465,000		28 weeks	29 Weeks
Database Migration Phase IV Project	↔	↔	↑	39%	275,000	110,000	281,250	4 Weeks	4 Weeks
E-Mail Migration Phase III	↓	↓	↓	59%	250,000	175,000		2 Weeks	2 Weeks
Voice Over IP Research Project	↑	↑	↔	48%	75,000	36,500	75,000	6 Weeks	6.5 Weeks
Employee Online Benefits Project	↓	↔	↓	57%	750,500	510,000		8 Weeks	13 Weeks

JenMar Dashboard Report

The first three (3) variables indicate performance against the traditional project management triangle. The arrow direction indicates performance as compared to the last reporting period. A down arrow indicates that the performance is worse than in the previous period, a sideways arrow indicates that performance is stable between the two periods, and an up arrow indicates that performance has improved since the last period. These indicators are only for variance in the three measures. The Cost EAC (Estimate At Completion) is a measure of how much the project is now expected to cost based on current performance. It is calculated by taking the (Cumulative Actual Costs) + (Total Budget - Cumulative Earned Value) / CPI. The Schedule EAC is a measure of how long the project is now expected to take based upon current performance. It is calculated by taking the original schedule / SPI (Schedule Performance Index).

Jim's Portfolio Dashboard Report

The dashboard showed each project listed on the far left side of the page. Across each row were a series of indicators that appeared as red, yellow or green dots. The projects were grouped based upon organizational departments. The column just to the right of the project name contained an indicator showing the project's current status. Additionally, there were columns representing the major strategic drivers for JenMar, who the project manager was, the priority, the start date, and the targeted completion date.

After a quick review of the dashboard Ken looked at Jim and asked, "As the senior executive of the organization, how are you using this report?"

Jim was quick to respond to this simple question, "This report is the primary oversight report for all active initiatives. I and the rest of the senior management team use it to see which initiatives need our attention and we use it to manage everyone's expectations."

"That makes sense," Ken responded. "But, how do you know which projects really need your attention?" Ken asked.

"That is what the first indicator is for," Jim responded. "A red indicator light indicates the project has significant problems. A yellow indicator means there are potential issues or warning signs on the project, and a green indicator means the project is on target."

Ken spent a few minutes asking about several of the other reports in front of him before asking if he could get a Coke. While Ken waited for the Coke to arrive he took another look at the portfolio indicator report and then asked Jim, "How is the status determined on each project?"

Jim was confused by Ken's question so he asked, "Do you mean the colored status indicators?"

"Yes, exactly," Ken responded.

"Well," Jim explained, "We use a brand new enterprise-wide project management software system to capture the status from each project manager."

Ken followed that question quickly with another, "And, how do they know what the current status is?"

At this point Jim really wasn't sure he understood where Ken was going with the conversation so he paused before answering. "I'm not sure I understand what you are driving at, but each project manager is trained on our definitions. If the project on target, we say it is in the green. If it will miss its target by a nominal amount it is yellow, and if the project will miss its target significantly we say it is in the red."

"That answers my question," Ken said. He then added, "But how do you decide if the project was completed successfully?"

"That's easy," Jim said. "We survey our customers. If they are not happy then we failed."

"Isn't that a little late?" Ken asked.

"What do you mean?" Jim responded.

"There are two main areas of management focus with which you and you management team must contend," Ken started. "These are doing the things to keep the basic business going, or operations, and the other is creating new products and services, or projects. There are a lot of similarities between the two, but there are also differences. Based on our previous discussions and the answers you gave me today, I think we need to stay focused on the new product or service development side if that is OK with you."

"Sure," Jim said.

"Customer satisfaction is an important indicator of success, but there are two problems with it," Ken began.

"First, customer satisfaction is both qualitative and subjective. This means it is very difficult to obtain a measure of it on which everyone agrees. If your customer happened to have a fight with their spouse before coming to work it is highly likely they will evaluate you lower than if something really great just happened. Secondly, customer satisfaction is typically a lagging indicator. This means it is only reviewed after the initiative has been completed. This means the results can only be responded to in a reactive mode. To truly impact results you must be able to respond to situations proactively, while problems are minor. Once the problems become large you have a very low probability of changing the outcome."

Ken waited for Jim and Catherine to confirm they were following what he was saying before continuing. "Jim, right now you have two primary indicators for performance on your major initiatives. These indicators are the status light you described and the customer satisfaction survey taken at the end. However, both of these indicators are highly qualitative and subjective and they are failing you."

Ken's last statement caused Jim to sit up in his chair. "How so?" he asked Ken.

"Well," Ken said. "Do you remember when we discussed the need to change the reporting information you were capturing from your teams?"

"Sure," Jim responded. "We changed to capturing the hours worked and remaining hours to get a better idea of the real results. Over the last few weeks we have really seen an improvement in the accuracy of our estimates without people inflating things, but what do these indicators have to do with our current discussion?"

"The way you used to do reporting represents another example of a qualitative and subjective metric. The difference is that the ones we are discussing now actually can be used when added after the quantitative metrics are established," Ken answered. "It is all about getting the organization to manage strategically instead of by crisis."

"That really piques my interest," Jim commented. "I know we have to get our people to think more long term, but how can we ever do it if we are always going from one brush fire to the next? At the end of the day we are just doing management by crisis and it is wearing everyone out."

"You are not alone," Ken responded. "In fact, you are just like most organizations. The problem is that you are measuring high level metrics without measuring the basics."

Now Jim was really confused. Hadn't Ken just said that subjective measures created problems, now he was calling them high level '*metrics*'. He could tell Catherine was not tracking either. In fact, she beat him to the punch. "Wait a minute," Catherine said. "You are not making any sense. Can you explain what you mean?"

"Sure," Ken responded. "What I mean is that measuring customer satisfaction is a good thing. It is a very good thing. However, a customer satisfaction measure will not improve customer satisfaction unless you are also measuring several basic quantitative metrics as well. This is because indicators such as customer satisfaction are lagging indicators. They only provide information after the fact which means they can't help you with any of the current initiatives. The results from satisfaction surveys are always reactive. The customer tells you they are unhappy with some result. The result is already there. You are just trying to repair the damage. To succeed you also have to have metrics that allow you to be proactive with the current initiatives, to help you solve problems when they are small before you are doing damage control and crisis management."

That made sense to both Jim and Catherine, but neither of them was sure how to implement what Ken was suggesting. "So what are you recommending we do?" Jim asked.

"Start by changing your basic performance report," Ken said. "Your current process causes you to focus all your attention on happy customers, but does nothing to help you attain those happy customers in a profitable way. How many times have you ever had a contract where the deal initially appeared great for JenMar, but somehow the profit just wasn't there when the contract closed?"

"I was just looking at several deals from last year yesterday with our Vice President of Sales where that was the case. We ended up spending so much in overtime completing the deal that we lost money on the deals, and on several other deals we were using salaried staff so it didn't cost us real money unless you consider the projects we didn't get done and the people we lost due to burnout."

"Exactly," Ken said. "The rule you have to remember is that late, over budget, technical successes are failures. You goal has to be to deliver on time, on budget what has been promised. To do that you must have every manager measuring their results against the planned schedule, budget and the scope."

"Wait a minute," Jim said. "Some of that financial information is pretty important. I am not sure we want every initiative manager having the salary information for all our staff."

"I am not suggesting you do that at all. All I am suggesting is that you establish a single or several pooled labor rates for the initiative resources; that you require each initiative to have a planned budget as well as a schedule; and that you consistently measure against those targets."

"OK, sounds reasonable," Jim said. "But, how are we to do that?"

"It is actually a lot easier than it sounds. Remember when I asked you to begin to collect the answers to two questions:

1. How many hours we spent on each deliverable?
2. How many hours are left to complete the deliverable?

With these two answers, you can calculate the major indicators. The most common variance standards consider a project being green if it is within 10% of target, yellow between 10% - 20% of target and red if the variance is greater than 20% of target. You will simply be calculating two variables: the Cost Performance Indicator or CPI; and the Schedule Performance Indicator or SPI from Earned Value Management. Once you begin to regularly hold your managers accountable to these indicators as well, your customer satisfaction surveys will have a lot more value because these new statistics will help you see problems and the surveys will tell you why there is a problem. Above all else, remember this is about probability and not precision."

"I think this is going to hard to implement with our people, but I see why it is so important," Jim said with a sigh. He then added, "but, I think this change is necessary. Ken can we meet again in about six weeks?"

"Sure," Ken replied.

With that Ken shook hands with Jim and Catherine and headed for the door. He looked at his watch as he headed for his car. Good, he thought. I am early. He had plenty of time to get home and change before taking his son to the Denver Nuggets basketball game that night. The Nuggets had traded for Chauncy Billups and the team was playing much better.

Strategic Alignment

It had only been three weeks since his last meeting when Ken ran into Jim at a dinner party held by a mutual friend. After about 30 minutes of small talk Jim said to Ken, "I think our joint efforts are running out of steam. We have been working together for almost nine months. I am grateful for all your advice, but I am not sure if we can get there from here."

Ken was taken aback for a moment and didn't quite know how to respond. Jim's recommendation carried a lot of weight in the community and Ken's business had really grown over the last year largely based on Ken's work with JenMar. If his big success story was no longer a success it might mean the end of a great ride. However, Jim had always been fair and a good friend so Ken hoped he could quickly get to the root of Jim's concern and turn it around. Ken asked Jim to explain further.

"First let me tell you how much I appreciate all you have done for JenMar. We have made huge progress because of your help, and I know we would not have made that progress if you had not been there to advise us. However, we are losing a lot of steam on the process changes we are making, and I feel like the senior management team is just spread too thin. I have already cancelled our Lean Initiative. It simply failed to deliver, and I am working with our CIO on what we can do to get our ITIL initiative back on solid footing. I am debating in my mind how our work together fits, and if it is pulling resources from other critical work."

"Wow," Ken said. "I really appreciate your openness and frankness Jim. Can we meet to address your concerns?"

"Absolutely," Jim said before adding, "I was hoping you would say that. Can we meet Thursday for lunch?"

"It's a date," Ken said. The two men settled on a place to meet before enjoying the rest of the evening.

Ken had spent the first three days of the week preparing for the meeting with Jim. Fortunately, Jim had allowed Catherine share any information Ken requested. After two days of wrestling with the information, Ken had finally seen the light, and he was pretty sure Jim would see it too. As he pulled into the restaurant parking lot Ken was feeling more confident than he had felt in several days. Jim was a friend, but more importantly, he was a savvy businessman.

Ken had a one page summary of the discussion prepared for Jim, but he waited to give it to him until he had made his case. After a few minutes of small talk Ken decided it was now or never.

"Jim, thanks for allowing your people to share all the information with me. It provided me with some great insights and I think I have found the solution to your problem."

Jim smiled. He also understood the stakes of this meeting. Although he would like to see his longtime friend succeed, JenMar was now looking to him for leadership so this would be strictly a business decision. However, he still hoped his friend could provide the answers he needed. JenMar was at least on stable footing now, but with recession in full swing that would not be enough. He nodded for Ken to continue.

Ken took a deep breath and started, "I took a look at all the changes we had discussed earlier and how you had implemented the changes. It looks like you successfully implemented each idea we discussed and after some initial resistance saw strong positive results. However, after the first five or six months JenMar's progress has ground to a halt. Based on the information I have been able to collect you have seen similar results with the other major improvement initiatives within the organization. At this point, you believe that JenMar is attempting too many changes too quickly, and it is time to slow down or you will lose all the progress you have already made. Am I on the right track?"

"I think you are pretty close," Jim said with a grimace.

"It took me a long time to understand the pattern," Ken continued. Now Ken had Jim's interest peaked. He very much wanted to understand the pattern Ken was suggesting.

Ken continued, "Over the years I have watched executives such as you struggle with organizational improvement initiatives and the same thing happens over and over again. It has not mattered what the initiatives were, from TQM, to Six Sigma, to Agile Six Sigma, to Lean, Project Management, ITIL, or Agile Development, the results have largely been the same. I think I told you before that my research shows seven out of ten of these efforts fail within 12 months and that on average organizations will invest over $750,000 to implement these ideas."

Jim recalled how he felt the first time he had heard Ken's numbers, and he did not like them any better after hearing them a second time. Jim knew JenMar was pretty close to those numbers on a couple of the initiatives Ken had mentioned. Then an idea struck him.

"Ken, are you sure organizations are not just improperly implementing these ideas? For example, ITIL, Six Sigma and Lean all have project management processes built into them. The project management standards such as those promoted by PMI® suggest that continuous process improvement is a key element of a quality knowledge area. It has always seemed to be a chicken or the egg argument in terms of which of these is dominant."

Ken had to smile at this comment. He knew Jim was correct in his analysis, but wanted to get Jim to the big idea. "Jim, I think you have it exactly right. Many of these processes can add value and improve organizational performance. Unfortunately, most start out strong only to quickly fade amidst frustration from leadership and worker alike. I am convinced the reason these efforts fail is because the people who actually have to implement these changes do not understand how their initiatives impacts the organizational strategy. When people fail to understand how their work aligns to the organizational strategy they do not commit to it and the initiative eventually loses steam as just another flavor of the month."

Jim thought for a moment and then said, "What you are describing is an engagement problem, and it does make some sense. My gut has been telling me for some time that JenMar probably had a number of people who were not fully committed to the changes we were trying to enact and were simply keeping their heads down and hoping the changes would blow over so they could keep doing things the way they always have. If you are right then it would not matter what methodology or process improvement initiative we tried they would all meet with the same end. If that is true, we are back to solving the ownership problem we discussed earlier."

After a moment's pause Jim asked, "Ken, suppose I believe in your idea. What can we do about it? If you're right won't any initiative fail?"

"That is the very idea that troubled me for a lot of nights. I mean think about all the business books that have been published touting different management philosophies. If this conclusion is right they are all a waste! Fortunately, I don't think that is the case. If you look carefully at the successful companies there is one consistency. These organizations are using the same ideas and techniques we have been working the past several months, but they also apply them to the organizational strategy. They establish quantitative metrics at the strategic level, usually in the form of a balanced scorecard, ensure every member of the organization understands how their work will lead to the achievement of the strategy and never stop measuring against those metrics. In the end it is all about aligning every resource to the strategy. If people do not understand how they fit into the strategy they cannot take ownership."

Ken stopped there and looked at Jim. He could not tell what Jim was thinking.

After thinking for a moment Jim finally spoke, "What you are saying makes a lot of sense and I think you might have something. Although I believe we probably were attempting too many ideas that had competing philosophies, I think the ones we keep would be a lot more successful if we implemented your idea. I'll tell you what, let me take your idea to my management team and if they are able to get results with it we will keep our contract open."

Ken had to smile. Jim's answer was the not a blanket endorsement, but it kept the door open. "Great. I also am more than willing to help your people with implementation, if it would be helpful."

Now it was Jim's turn to smile. "Ken was still a consultant, wasn't he?" Jim thought. "Sure," Jim said. "I'll have Catherine give you a call this afternoon and you two can work together to get this done, but I want to make sure you understand there is not much room for error here. If we do not see a return on investment we are going to have to move in a different direction."

"I completely understand, and Jim, thanks for the opportunity. I am sure you are going to be pleased with the results."

With that the two friends shook hands, Ken left and Jim returned to his desk to look over the plans for JenMar's new product line.

Process Won't Get You There. People Will

It had been over a month since Ken had met with Jim. In that time Ken and Catherine had spent a lot of time with JenMar's senior management team implementing Ken's idea. It was made easier because Jim had implemented a formal strategic planning process complete with a balanced scorecard when he had first come on board. In fact, most of Ken and Catherine's time had been spent creating a process that would ensure every person on JenMar's staff clearly understood how they impacted the organizational strategy and how the various process initiatives helped achieve the desired results.

After what appeared to be a lack of interest by a few people, and only feigned participation by others most of the organization had come to realize the importance of their own work to the company's success and had become eager participants. However, not everything had gone perfectly. After only a few weeks Ken and Catherine had found a couple of people who were simply unwilling to change or engage with the rest of the organization.

Fortunately, Catherine had taken the lead in these situations and those resources were being put on performance plans and/or coached out of the company. Ken remembered what his old grad school professor had always told him, "Everyone is bound to be great somewhere, some people just won't be great with you. For those people it is important that you release them to their destiny."

Ken was excited to meet with Jim today. He was also a little nervous. Although they had been very successful, he and Catherine had also run into a problem. Over the last several weeks they had been constantly working to develop a robust process, yet no matter how much time they spent with it they kept running into JenMar team members who provided valid concerns about the process needing rules and processes for specific exceptions. It was really beginning to get maddening. That was alright though. Even with this problem, JenMar was back on track. The numbers didn't lie. It was now very likely that in the next 12 months JenMar would take over the number one market position.

After walking Jim through the new processes and the results to-date Ken stopped and asked if Jim had any questions or concerns.

"No," Jim replied. He had been getting regular status reports from Catherine and was very pleased with the results. So much so that he wanted Ken to agree to a six month contract extension.

After Ken agreed Jim asked, "So do you see any challenges which I should know about?"

"Actually there is one," Ken responded, and he outlined the exception problem that had been frustrating both he and Catherine. This time it was Jim's turn to smile. As many times as Ken had been the one to provide Jim with help with a problem it was nice to see Ken was human after all and didn't have every answer.

"I think I can help you with that one," Jim said.

 "I am all ears," Ken responded.

"Ken, after all my years as an executive the one thing I have learned is there is no such thing as a perfect process. What you are trying to create is a process that will work for at least 80% of the cases, and understand there will always exceptions. The real key to success is not the processes you use. The only way you can succeed is to take care of your people. In the end it comes down to being a servant leader."

"Servant leader," Ken responded. "I have never heard of that term. What does it mean?"

"The term was originally coined by Robert Greenleaf in his book by the same name. I guess the easiest way to understand it is to think about the traditional management pyramid," Jim started.

"In the traditional model the organization is organized like a pyramid with each organizational level working to serve the needs and direction set by the level above it until you reach the single person at the top. In simplest terms a servant leader is one who inverts this pyramid and believes the organization will best succeed if they focus on lifting each of the people beneath them. I truly believe that the very best leaders focus on serving even the very lowest members of their organization. As JenMar's CEO I do very little real work. In fact, I seem to spend most of my time in meetings talking about other people doing work. My people actually deliver the results.

Unfortunately, most organizations end up with a very strong process orientation. While structure and process are both very important they cannot ever replace the need for a core focus on the people within the organization."

"Wow!" Ken said. "I have always told people you were great with people, but I always thought it was just a personality thing with you. I now see the philosophy that makes you so successful."

Jim had to smile at that. He always considered himself more of a technician, an engineer. It was good to know he could still teach his old friend a thing or two.

"Just remember," Jim added after a brief pause. "We are not trying to create automatons. We are trying to build leaders. Like any organization, the only way we can succeed long-term is if we develop real leaders at every level of the company who we trust with the authority to make command decisions. We will never be able to do that through some process."

"I could not agree more," Ken responded. "We just have to make sure our process institutionalizes your philosophy."

"Exactly," Jim said, and the quickly added, "I think you have some adjustments to make don't you?"

Ken agreed. He left Jim's office energized about the changes that needed to be made.

A New Reality

It had been several months since Ken had been out to see Jim Calvin, and a lot had changed for Ken and his small consulting practice. Jim's advice had led to revolution in Ken's thinking which Ken had combined with the basic leadership tenants he had been teaching for years to create his new management philosophy. He was now working to complete a book teaching his seven major ideas. These ideas included:

1. People Change Easily, But Are Difficult To Change
2. First Define The What Then Define The How
3. Manage Deliverables Not Tasks
4. Manage Starts Not Finishes
5. Performance Metrics
6. Late, Over Budget Technical Successes Are Failures
7. The Need for Strategic Alignment

The major insight Ken had found thanks to Jim was that no matter how robust and well thought out his process thinking was, it all came down to people. To be successful, managers had to shift their thinking and invert the pyramid. The more Ken thought about it the more obvious it became. The difference between great leaders and mediocre leaders was found in their ability to remove any process that prevented their people from being successful. Great leaders, it seemed, always assumed positive intent. By assuming positive intent a leader could focus on creating processes that did not turn the organization into automatons and instead created an organization of robust, thinking resources capable of solving almost any problem.

After several months of thought on this concept, Ken finally settled on three rules he was sure would help organizations be successful.

1. Everyone needs to know the numbers.
2. People need to run efforts like they own them.
3. The organization must be directionally correct.

When Ken first tested these rules with several of his clients he met with some resistance. In fact, one client thought it was one of the most dangerous ideas they had heard. After all, it was highly likely that their competition would learn the numbers as well. However, Ken had eventually won them over as well by continually focusing on the need of every organization's resources to take ownership of the corporate strategy and arguing that would not happen if people did not understand the numbers.

Several of Ken's clients had even more difficulty with his second rule. It seemed that many executives were simply not comfortable pushing control and authority down to the people actually doing the work. After a couple of difficult cases, Ken had concluded the root of this problem lay in the fear of not having any control over the objective to which the executive was being held accountable. It took a while, but Ken finally was able to convince these leaders to push authority down to every level of the organization by explaining to these executives that they were not actually giving up control. By establishing strong, quantitative performance metrics and pushing authority to the every level of the organization they would actually have more control and accountability than ever before.

Ken's third rule, you must be directionally correct, was the most difficult to get his clients to accept. However, it was the most important. This rule establishes the basic organizational understanding that no one is perfect and mistakes will happen. The key is to ensure proper risk management occurs and then share the key learning from each mistake throughout the entire organization so mistakes are not repeated. A few of Ken's clients were not comfortable with this idea, and it definitely went against many organizational cultures where mistakes were quickly brushed under the rug, blame was quickly placed and lessons had to be learned repeatedly. When Ken showed his clients how many times the organization was making the same mistakes they usually got the point quickly.

In addition to writing his first book, Ken was now spending a significant amount of his time speaking to groups about his ideas. This was the part of the business he really loved. He always seemed to get energized by talking to people about how to improve their organizations. His audiences were now consistently growing as more and more companies were struggle to find ways to improve the organization in lean times.

Whenever he spoke to company leaders he was amazed at the frustration many of them were feeling at the lack of results from these efforts and how many others could not provide a good answer when Ken asked how they knew the results were what they thought. In the end, each of these organizations was just going through the revolving door of processes that created the <u>Flavor of the Month</u>.

The more organizations he visited the more Ken was convinced his simple ideas could improve any process and any organization.

Ken had to smile as he and his son boarded the flight. Thanks to the real business results from his ideas he was taking his son to the Super Bowl. Now he just had to figure out what he was going to do for his wife.